TRY AGAIN: The Road to WHOLEness in 30 Days

Dr. Casaundra Monique McNair

Try Again by Dr. Casaundra "Monique" McNair

Copyright © 2025 by Casaundra M. McNair; The McNair Co.

All rights reserved. No part of this book may be reproduced or transmitted in any form or by any means, electronic or mechanical, including photocopying, recording, or by any information storage and retrieval system without written permission of the author.

All verses quoted are from the New Living Translation of the Bible unless otherwise noted.

Library of Congress Cataloging-in-Publication Data
By: Casaundra M. McNair
Try Again: The Road to Wholeness in 30 Days.

ISBN 978-0-9993973-4-3

www.themcnairco.org

Cover Design: Dee Shervell

DEDICATION

To God, the ultimate author of my story… Thank You for every closed door that led to greater opportunities, every delay that built my faith, and every challenge that shaped my purpose. Your plans are always greater than my own.

To my husband who was built for me… our children and loved ones, whose prayers, love, and unwavering support have been my anchor in every season. Your encouragement has reminded me that even when the path is uncertain, I am never walking alone.

To those who, like me, have faced unexpected changes, disappointments, or moments of doubt—this book is for you. May you find the courage to stand up, press forward, and TRY AGAIN… Because God is not finished with you yet! Be healed and be WHOLE!

TABLE OF CONTENTS

INTRODUCTION	i
Day 1- Face the Truth	1
Day 2- Blurred Vision	5
Day 3- End Negative Self-Talk	9
Day 4- Release the Hurt	13
Day 5- Release the Pain	17
Day 6- Change Your Mindset	21
Day 7- Change Your Routine	25
Day 8- Be Healed	29
Day 9- Define Your Focus	33
Day 10- Goal Setting	37
Day 11- Define Your Vision	41
Day 12- Be Accountable	45
Day 13- Speak What You Know	49
Day 14- Discouragement	53
Day 15- Friends	57
Day 16- Posture of Prayer	61
Day 17- Fueled with Faith	65
Day 18- Restoration of Ideas	69

Day 19- End Procrastination	73
Day 20- So What?	77
Day 21- Knowledge Plus Experience…	81
Day 22- Don't Let the Past Creep Up on You	85
Day 23- Handle Business	89
Day 24- Swift Obedience	93
Day 25- Grow Where You are Planted	97
Day 26- Impatience	101
Day 27- Are you Prepared?	105
Day 28- Calibrating for Continual Success	109
Day 29- Pay it Forward	113
Day 30- Redeem the Time	117
WHAT'S NEXT	121

INTRODUCTION

Have you ever woke up to a mile-long to-do list and felt frozen by the sheer weight of it all? Maybe you carefully planned every step toward your goals—whether in your career, family life, finances, or spiritual journey—yet everything unraveled because of circumstances you couldn't control. Frustration sets in, and you start questioning: Why can't the people around me see I need help? Why won't they support me? Is my breakthrough ever going to happen?

I've been there... many times. Early in my life, I longed for change but had no blueprint to follow. No one in my family had ventured beyond a high school diploma, some college; no one had navigated single parenthood or at least ever talked openly about the roadblocks that threaten to derail us from fulfilling our God-given dreams. Without guidance, at times... I felt bound, tied down by invisible limitations I couldn't name. Each time I tried to move forward—whether by pursuing higher education, improving my finances, or nurturing my spiritual walk—I'd falter. It was as if I were caught in a cycle of hoping, trying, and failing, wondering if something in me was fundamentally broken.

Yet, the beautiful truth is that God has a knack for showing up in our darkest hours with a word that changes everything. One day, in the midst of my frustration and discouragement, I heard Him whisper:

"TRY AGAIN." It was a simple but profound invitation to embrace a new mindset. Suddenly, scriptures that I'd read countless times began to make sense in a deeper way, like Proverbs 24:16, which says, "Though the righteous fall seven times, they rise again." If God calls us righteous, it's not because we never fail, but because we keep getting up. And so I did. Slowly, I realized that genuine success isn't about perfect execution on the first attempt. Rather, it's about learning, adjusting, and pressing forward each time you stumble.

It wasn't an overnight transformation, but more of a continuous, day-by-day surrender. I learned that failure can actually be a faithful teacher, revealing where we need to recalibrate our plans, strengthen our relationships, and deepen our trust in God. Think of James 1:2-4, which encourages us to consider trials "an opportunity for great joy" because the testing of our faith produces perseverance. It's in these rocky moments—when you're forced to "try again" that spiritual stamina is built.

That's exactly why this 30-day journey to WHOLEness exists. It's for people who, like me, are convinced there's more to life—more to them—but feel stuck in cycles of near-successes and repeated setbacks. Over the next month, you'll embark on a purposeful expedition through Scriptures, reflection prompts, and tangible action steps. You'll learn to align your daily choices with God's will, fortify your faith, and overcome obstacles—both internal and external—in your family, career, and ministry. Jeremiah 29:11 boldly reminds us that God's plans for us are good, "to give you a future and a hope," even when circumstances suggest otherwise.

As you dive into these devotionals, you might confront old memories, fears, and insecurities that have hindered your progress. Let me encourage you with Isaiah 43:19: "Behold, I am doing a new thing... do you not perceive it?" God stands ready to breathe fresh life into your weary dreams, if you'll allow Him. Just as a seed must break open before it sprouts, your seeming 'brokenness' can be the very doorway to a season of unprecedented growth. Don't let past failures or the opinions of others define what God has already declared possible for you.

So, do yourself a favor: decide right now that you will try again. Make an unwavering commitment to invest in your future—spiritually, emotionally, and practically. As you read each day's devotional, reflect on the key Scriptures, and put these principles into practice, keep these two words at the forefront:

- TRY: Make an attempt or effort to do something.
- AGAIN: Once more—especially after you've gained insight from what didn't work before.

It's possible you won't get it exactly right the first time, or the second—or even the seventh. But each small step forward is a testimony of resilience, a nod to the transforming power of God's grace. Remember Galatians 6:9, which encourages us not to grow weary in doing good, for "at the proper time we will reap a harvest if we do not give up." Every setback you face can become a stepping stone, a lesson pointing you toward a fresh approach or a renewed heart posture. Instead of an ending, these moments become the prologue to a new beginning.

What if the perceived delays in your life are actually divine opportunities to strengthen your character, sharpen your gifts, and grow closer to the Lord? As Romans 8:28 affirms, God works "all things" for the good of those who love Him. If you truly believe that, then every hurdle—no matter how daunting—carries the seed of future triumph. 2 Timothy 1:7 reminds us that "God has not given us a spirit of fear," so you don't have to remain shackled by what once held you back.

Take heart. There is a beautiful, uncharted depth to you that God is eager to unveil through this journey. Each day, you'll focus on a new aspect of growth—from releasing hurts and ending negative self-talk, to refining your vision and setting actionable goals. Through Scripture, real-life applications, and guided reflections, you'll discover that the life of WHOLEness you've longed for is entirely within reach.

So, are you ready? Pause, take a breath, and give yourself permission to start anew. Let go of the old cycles, regrets, and what-ifs. Embrace the truth: God has destined you for more than mere survival; He desires for you to thrive and shine, reflecting His goodness to those around you. It's time to try again—and keep trying—

until you see the fullness of the promise He's placed over your life.

Let's begin this 30-day journey together, stepping boldly into the path of WHOLEness that God has designed just for you. Remember, "The steadfast love of the Lord never ceases; His mercies never come to an end; they are new every morning" (Lamentations 3:22-23). With each dawn, God offers you a fresh start—a chance to rise, recommit, and walk in victory. Let's seize that gift, day by day, and discover the transformation that awaits.

DAY 1: FACE THE TRUTH

Scriptures

- You are made in the image of God (Matthew 10:29-31)
- You are fearfully and wonderfully made (Psalm 139:14)
- "Committed and persistent work pays off; get-rich-quick schemes are ripoffs." (Proverbs 28:20 MSG)

Devotion

Commitment and success go hand in hand. If you don't commit, you don't succeed. Yet for many of us, commitment is daunting because it demands persistence, discipline, and sometimes change. We can be so afraid of failing—or even of succeeding—that we avoid stepping into new territory altogether. Jeremiah 29:11 reminds us that God's thoughts toward us are for peace, not evil, and that He has a future, and a hope prepared for us. But we won't see that future fully unless we are willing to face what's directly in front of us. Perhaps it's a difficult decision about your career, an unresolved conflict in a relationship, or simply the fear of leaving your comfort zone. Whatever it is, know that staying honest about your present situation—while trusting God's promises—paves the way for true, lasting success.

"Good success," in biblical terms, isn't about accolades, wealth, or status. It's about walking in God's will. You can climb every ladder and conquer every project in your own strength, but without abiding in Him, you'll still feel empty. The real question becomes: Am I seeking God's direction, or am I chasing my own idea of success rooted in worldly values? If you're uncertain, bring that question to prayer. Remember that God is faithful to guide a willing heart. The moment you decide to align with His will and trust His leading, you'll find a peace that surpasses human understanding—even if the road ahead looks unfamiliar.

Ultimately, success isn't about doing more; it's about becoming more—becoming the person God created you to be. It may require confronting tough realities or letting go of old habits. But with every step of faith, you'll discover that God has already gone before you, setting each piece of the puzzle in place. When you commit wholeheartedly to Him, you let go of the pressure to measure up to the world's standards. Instead, you'll rest in the knowledge that His plan and His timing are perfect.

Questions for Reflection

1. What prayers have I prayed for God to reveal my true self?
2. What scriptures or promises from God am I standing on today?
3. In what ways can I align my definition of success more closely with God's perspective?

_____
_____
_____
_____
_____
_____
_____
_____

_____
_____
_____
_____
_____
_____
_____
_____
_____
_____
_____
_____
_____

Prayer for Today

Father, I thank You for Your goodness and grace. Thank You for still being God despite my disappointments. Help me become the person You have ordained me to be. Reveal Your will for my life. I lay aside every weight and sin that so easily holds me back. Forgive me for doing my own thing instead of following Your way. Fill every void in my life with Your presence. In Jesus' name, amen.

Self-Affirmation

I will not allow others' perceptions of me to override the truth of who God created me to be.

DAY 2: BLURRED VISION

Scripture

"So let's keep focused on that goal, those of us who want everything God has for us. If any of you have something else in mind, something less than total commitment, God will clear your blurred vision—you'll see it yet! Now that we're on the right track, let's stay on it." (Philippians 3:15-16 MSG)

Devotion

On the road to trying, some days it seems like you can't get ahead—no matter how hard you push or how many times you pray. You might look around at your finances, relationships, or spiritual life and feel overwhelmed, wondering how you ended up in a tough situation or how you'll ever get out of it. Sometimes, when you're knee-deep in adversity, it's hard to see the "exit route." Emotions like fear, disappointment, or frustration can blur your vision, making it even more challenging to discern God's leading. You might even find yourself questioning whether God is still present, or if He's grown silent just when you need Him most.

When your vision is blurred by pain or confusion, you can easily miss the divine appointments and open doors God has placed right in front of you. Like someone squinting through fog, you sense something is there but can't fully make it out. However, Jeremiah 33:3 reminds us that when we call out to the Lord, He promises to show us great and mighty things—things we wouldn't see otherwise. This promise encourages us to pray fervently for clarity and perspective. God isn't holding out on you; He delights in revealing the path forward when you genuinely seek Him. In the same way that physical fog eventually lifts, spiritual clarity arrives when we invite the Holy Spirit to illuminate our circumstances.

Blurred vision can also tempt us to compare our journey to others, feeding a sense of inadequacy or envy. Resist that urge. God's plan for you is as unique as your fingerprint. Instead, fix your eyes on Jesus, "the author and finisher of our faith" (Hebrews 12:2). Lean into Scriptures that remind you of His faithfulness and surround yourself with a community of believers who can pray with you and speak truth into your life. Remember, when you ask Him for guidance, He can—and will—clear your blurred vision, allowing you to see both the path ahead and the blessings He's strategically placed in your life.

Questions for Reflection

1. How am I viewing my current situation?
2. Do I believe that God sees it differently? If so, how?
3. In what specific ways can I invite God to bring clarity and lift the spiritual fog in my life?

_____

_____

_____

_____

_____

_____

_____

Prayer for Today

Lord, please help me remain focused and see my life the way You see it. Remove any blurred vision caused by worry, fear, or doubt. Guide me onto the right track and keep my feet firmly planted in Your truth. Amen.

Self-Affirmation

I see myself according to the Word of God, and I will stay on the path He has set for me.

DAY 3: END NEGATIVE SELF-TALK

Scripture

"Death and life are in the power of the tongue, and those who love it and indulge it will eat its fruit and bear the consequences of their words." (Proverbs 18:21 AMP)

Devotion

Our words shape our realities in profound ways. Imagine you're cooking a meal: before you even break out the pots and pans, you mentally list the ingredients and decide whether you have what it takes to finish well. If you assume you can't pull it off, you're likely to quit or cut corners before you even begin. Spiritually and emotionally, the same pattern follows us. When we repeatedly say, "I can't," "I'm not good enough," or "It'll never work," we end up living under the shadow of those declarations. Our internal dialogue becomes a self-fulfilling prophecy, limiting how we see ourselves and what we believe God can do through us.

But Proverbs 18:21 reminds us that "death and life are in the power of the tongue," underscoring that our words carry real spiritual weight. If we choose to believe God's truth instead—that we are loved, chosen, and capable through Christ—our words begin to shift. Every time you declare "I can do all things through Christ who strengthens me" (Philippians 4:13) in the face of doubt, you're realigning your perspective with God's promises. It doesn't magically erase difficulties, but it does awaken a sense of hope and possibility. Over time, this shift in language feeds your faith, empowering you to take bold steps in your spiritual journey.

It's important to remember that speaking life goes beyond self-affirmation; it's about partnering with God's Word to shape our thinking. Ask the Holy Spirit to highlight any lingering negative labels or self-defeating phrases you've grown used to saying. Then, consciously replace them with Scriptures or biblically grounded affirmations. Let your words become a testimony to the transforming power of Christ—proof that even the toughest challenges can be met with faith and expectation. The more you align your language with God's heart, the more you'll see your life and mindset transformed, one declaration at a time.

Questions for Reflection

1. What self-defeating statements or negative labels have I spoken over myself?

2. How can I replace these words with God's truth and promises?

3. In what ways might shifting my internal dialogue impact my overall faith and daily decisions?

Prayer for Today

Lord, help me see myself as You see me. Cancel every negative word I've spoken over my life. Replace it with words of faith and affirmation that align with Your heart and promises. Amen.

Self-Affirmation

Choose your own life verse and create a daily affirmation. For example: "I am capable, I am loved, and I am walking in God's grace."

DAY 4: RELEASE THE HURT

Scripture

"Look after each other so that none of you fails to receive the grace of God. Watch out that no poisonous root of bitterness grows up to trouble you, corrupting many." (Hebrews 12:15 NLT)

Devotion

Hurt can sometimes hide beneath layers of bitterness. Like a tiny seed, it can take root and grow until it shapes our attitude toward life, relationships, and even how we perceive God. When you carry unresolved hurt, it not only affects you personally—manifesting as anger, resentment, or withdrawal—but it can also spill over into your conversations, decisions, and day-to-day interactions. You may find yourself lashing out at loved ones, sabotaging new opportunities, or feeling distant from God because a part of your heart remains wounded.

Releasing hurt is an intentional act that requires honest self-examination and deep surrender. Hebrews 12:15 warns us to watch out "that no poisonous root of bitterness grows up to trouble you, corrupting many." This verse underscores that bitterness doesn't just harm the person who harbors it; it spreads, affecting the people and environment around us. Allow God's grace to flood those secret places where you've been wounded—childhood pain, betrayal by a friend, or the heartbreak of unmet expectations. As you acknowledge your hurt before God, He can bring genuine healing and freedom. Forgiveness, both of yourself and others, becomes a powerful key that unlocks the fullness of God's love. Holding on to hurt keeps you from experiencing the peace and wholeness He desires for you. But the moment you release it into His capable hands, you'll discover that His power is made perfect in your weakness (2 Corinthians 12:9), ushering you into deeper healing than you ever thought possible.

Questions for Reflection

1. What past or recent hurts might still be affecting my decisions and relationships?

2. In what ways have I possibly allowed bitterness to take root?

3. How can I invite God's grace into those wounded areas so I can experience deeper healing and freedom?

_____
_____
_____
_____
_____
_____
_____
_____
_____
_____
_____
_____
_____
_____

Prayer for Today

Father, I lay my hurt and bitterness at Your feet. I no longer want to carry the weight of old wounds. Help me recognize where I've allowed bitterness to grow and give me the strength to release it to You. Amen.

Self-Affirmation

I am free from bitterness. I will allow God's love to replace every hurt with healing.

DAY 5: RELEASE THE PAIN

Scripture

"I am suffering and in pain. Rescue me, O God, by your saving power." (Psalm 69:29 NLT)

Devotion

Pain, when left unaddressed, often breeds more pain. It can manifest as anger, resentment, anxiety, or even self-sabotage, creating a cycle that's difficult to break. Acknowledging your pain is not weakness; rather, it's the vital first step toward true healing. Sometimes, we avoid confronting our hurts because we fear reopening old wounds or feeling vulnerable all over again. But pushing it aside can allow pain to grow in the shadows, influencing our thoughts, decisions, and relationships without us realizing it.

God is fully aware of every wound, every disappointment, and every moment you've felt alone in your struggle. Psalm 147:3 states, "He heals the brokenhearted and binds up their wounds." God cares deeply and offers both rescue and restoration, even when you can't see a way out. Your vulnerability before Him becomes a place where His power is made perfect, because it's in our moments of greatest need that we most profoundly experience His comforting presence. Allow yourself to bring each hurt, worry, and wound into the light of His love. As you do, trust that His grace is sufficient not just to carry you through the pain, but to heal it at the root.

Questions for Reflection

1. In what ways have I tried to ignore or numb my pain?
2. Do I truly believe God can rescue me and bring healing?

3. What practical steps—such as prayer, counseling, or sharing with a trusted mentor—can I take to confront my pain instead of avoiding it?

_____
_____
_____
_____
_____
_____
_____
_____
_____
_____
_____
_____
_____
_____
_____
_____
_____
_____
_____
_____

Prayer for Today

Lord, I give You my pain and ask You to transform it into purpose. Teach me not to run from my suffering but to bring it to the cross where You carried all sorrows. Thank You for being my ultimate rescuer and healer. In Jesus' name, amen.

Self-Affirmation

Pain does not define me. I am defined by the love and healing power of God.

DAY 6: CHANGE YOUR MINDSET

Scripture

"Therefore, if any man be in Christ, he is a new creature: old things are passed away; behold, all things are become new." (2 Corinthians 5:17 KJV)

Devotion

A growth mindset believes there is always room to learn, adapt, and evolve. A fixed mindset, on the other hand, might say, "I've never succeeded at this before, so I'll never succeed." Yet in Christ, you are continually renewed. Romans 12:2 encourages us to be transformed by the renewing of our minds, which means that even if you've been stuck in a certain perspective or pattern, you can shift that thinking through God's power. Like a child hitting new developmental milestones, there is no limit in God's kingdom to how far you can grow when you embrace a posture of learning and faith.

When the Bible says that old things pass away (2 Corinthians 5:17), it includes the negative labels and destructive patterns that may have once defined you. God makes all things new when you choose to see yourself through His transformative power. Each day, you have the opportunity to renew your mind with His truth and to walk in the grace He provides. Even small acts of faith—like trying something you once believed impossible—can become catalysts for tremendous personal and spiritual development. Embrace the invitation to trust that God has more for you than a life limited by old mindsets.

Questions for Reflection

1. In what areas of life am I most prone to a fixed mindset?
2. How can a focus on growth and renewal in Christ change my outlook?
3. What practical steps can I take this week to cultivate a growth mindset in my spiritual life?

_____
_____
_____
_____
_____
_____
_____
_____
_____
_____
_____
_____
_____
_____
_____
_____

Prayer for Today

Lord, renew my mind daily. Help me to see the possibilities rather than the limitations. Show me that with Your strength, I can grow beyond my past. Amen.

Self-Affirmation

I embrace a growth mindset, trusting God to transform every part of my life.

DAY 7: CHANGE YOUR ROUTINE- MAKE EVERY MOMENT COUNT

Scripture

Read Ecclesiastes 3:1-15 (NLT) reviewing the three key points.
- A Time for Everything
- God's Sovereignty over Seasons
- Eternity in Our Hearts

Devotion

There is a season for everything: joy and sorrow, building and tearing down, laughter and tears. Ecclesiastes 3 paints a vivid picture of life's ebbs and flows—revealing that each phase has its own purpose and lesson. When we understand this rhythm, we begin to recognize that time is a gift from God. How we steward that gift can mean the difference between stagnation and steady growth. Perhaps this is a season of preparation where you need to invest more time in study, or a season of rest where you learn to prioritize your mental and spiritual health. Regardless of your current situation, trusting God's timing and being intentional with how you spend your days can bring clarity and fruitfulness.

Take a moment to examine your daily schedule. Are you using your time wisely, or are distractions—like unnecessary tasks or endless social media scrolling—stealing precious moments? One practical change—such as limiting screen time—can yield hours that can be reinvested in prayer, creative pursuits, family time, or self-improvement. The key is to identify where your time is leaking away and prayerfully realign your daily habits with God's priorities. As you do, you'll discover a renewed sense of purpose and a deeper appreciation for the season you're in, even if it looks different from what you expected.

Questions for Reflection

1. What daily habits or routines are wasting my time?

2. How can I better manage my schedule to make room for growth?

3. Which season of life do I believe I'm in right now, and how can I honor God through it?

_____
_____
_____
_____
_____
_____
_____
_____
_____
_____
_____
_____

Prayer for Today

Lord, help me to value my days and use them wisely. Reveal where my time is being drained by unproductive habits and guide me to align my schedule with Your priorities. Amen.

Self-Affirmation

I guard my time, make every moment count, and focus on what truly matters.

DAY 8: BE HEALED!

Scripture

"He heals the brokenhearted and binds up their wounds." (Psalm 147:3 NIV)

Devotion

Healing is a journey, not a moment. It involves allowing God into the depths of our hearts where pain, trauma, or disappointment reside. Genuine healing often begins with the honest confession, "Lord, I'm broken, and I need You." Admitting our brokenness is not a sign of defeat but an invitation for God to work powerfully in our lives. When you take that brave step of vulnerability, you create space for God's comfort, wisdom, and transforming grace to flow in.

Be patient with the process. Sometimes healing unfolds in layers; as one wound closes, the Holy Spirit may gently reveal another area needing restoration. This doesn't mean you've failed or regressed; it means God loves you enough to ensure every part of your heart receives His tender care. Isaiah 61:3 speaks of God bestowing "a crown of beauty instead of ashes," reminding us that He can turn our deepest sorrows into markers of His goodness. Each day, surrender your hurts, fears, and doubts to Him. Let His perfect love stitch together every wound, replacing sorrow with joy, fear with faith, and brokenness with wholeness.

Questions for Reflection

1. What areas of my life remain unhealed because I've hesitated to open them to God?
2. How would my life change if I embraced healing fully?

3. What practical steps—prayer, community support, counseling—can I take this week to invite God's healing into every layer of my life?

_____

Prayer for Today

Father, I open my heart to Your healing power. Touch every broken place. Restore me to wholeness in Your presence. Thank You for loving me enough to heal my deepest wounds. In Jesus' name, amen.

Self-Affirmation

I am healed from the inside out. God's love restores and makes me whole.

DAY 9: DEFINE YOUR FOCUS

Scripture

"But seek first the kingdom of God and His righteousness, and all these things shall be added to you." (Matthew 6:33 NKJV)

Devotion

When life is chaotic, it's easy to scatter your attention in a hundred different directions. Responsibilities at work, family obligations, social events, and the constant buzz of technology can pull you in ways that leave you feeling both overwhelmed and unfulfilled. Defining your focus means putting God's kingdom first—allowing His priorities to shape yours. Matthew 6:33 reminds us to "seek first the kingdom of God," suggesting that our spiritual alignment should precede everything else.

If you chase every distraction or worldly goal, you'll likely find yourself perpetually behind and unsatisfied. That's because those pursuits, while not necessarily bad in themselves, don't have the power to fulfill your deepest need for purpose and direction. When your spiritual life is centered on God, other pieces in your life start aligning in unexpected but life-giving ways. Take a moment to write down your top three life priorities—do they truly reflect what God has been speaking to your heart? Invite the Holy Spirit to reveal areas where you may be chasing the temporal at the expense of the eternal. Remember, Psalm 37:4 promises that when we delight in the Lord, He will shape the desires of our hearts. Aligning your focus with His will positions you to live with greater peace, clarity, and momentum.

Questions for Reflection

1. Where have I placed my attention lately—on God's will or on temporary pursuits?

2. What is one tangible way I can center my day around seeking God first?

3. How might my life change if I consistently made God's kingdom and His purposes my primary focus?

_____
_____
_____
_____
_____
_____
_____
_____
_____
_____
_____
_____
_____
_____

Prayer for Today

Lord, I want my life's focus to be on You. Show me how to organize my tasks and ambitions around Your kingdom priorities. Keep me from distractions and help me align my heart with Yours. Amen.

Self-Affirmation

I focus on God first, trusting that He will order every other aspect of my life.

DAY 10: GOAL SETTING

Scripture

"Write the vision and make it plain on tablets, that he may run who reads it." (Habakkuk 2:2 NKJV)

Devotion

Setting goals is an act of faith. You're taking the vision God has placed in your heart and breaking it down into actionable steps. In Habakkuk 2:2, the prophet is instructed to "write the vision" so it's clear—an invitation to move beyond vague desires into concrete plans. When you put your goals on paper, you create a roadmap for accountability and progress. Think of it as partnering with God: you honor His guidance by outlining your intentions, and then you trust Him to direct your steps, provide resources, and open the right doors in His perfect timing.

Whether it's a personal goal—like a fitness or education milestone—or a spiritual one, such as deeper Bible study or ministry involvement, clarity is key. Visualizing your goal and praying over it daily can spark the motivation you need to keep going, even when obstacles arise. Proverbs 16:3 says, "Commit your work to the Lord, and your plans will be established." Involve God in each stage—brainstorming, planning, executing—and watch how He blesses your diligence. When you feel stuck, remember that He is more invested in your growth and success than you could ever be. Let Him lead, but also do your part to remain disciplined, faithful, and open to the ways He might refine or redirect your plans along the way.

Questions for Reflection

1. What goals has God placed on my heart that I've been hesitating to formalize?

2. Have I written them down and prayed over them specifically?

3. Who can I invite into my journey—whether a mentor, friend, or accountability partner—to help me stay focused and faithful?

Prayer for Today

Father, help me to set clear goals aligned with Your will. Give me the discipline to follow through and the faith to trust You with every step. Amen.

Self-Affirmation

My goals are clear, and I am empowered by God to achieve them.

DAY 11: VISION & PRAYER BOARDS

Scripture

"Where there is no vision, the people perish." (Proverbs 29:18 KJV)

Devotion

A vision board is a tangible, visual expression of your dreams and goals—a snapshot of where you believe God is taking you. As you collect images, words, and Scriptures that resonate with your heart, you're crafting more than just a collage; you're building a faith-based reminder of God's promises. Habakkuk 2:2 exhorts us to "write the vision and make it plain," suggesting that clarity is a crucial step in turning vision into reality. By making your dreams visible, you'll see daily inspiration to keep pressing forward, even when challenges arise.

Creating a vision board isn't a magical shortcut to success, but rather a hands-on way to stay mindful of God's leading. Invite Holy Spirit to guide you as you choose each picture or word. Ask Him to show you areas of your life where you may need greater faith, deeper trust, or a renewed commitment to His plan. Remember, your ultimate goal isn't just to achieve personal milestones but to align your pursuits with God's purpose for you.

A prayer board functions much like a vision board, but with a specific emphasis on your prayer requests and intercessions for the year. Instead of focusing on broad dreams or goals, you'll be collecting and posting the needs you want to lift before God—whether personal, family-related, community-oriented, or global concerns. By writing these prayer needs down and displaying them in a visible place, you create a habit of praying with intentionality. Each time you walk by and see the list of requests, it serves as a prompt to engage in conversation with God, lifting those needs continually before Him.

Over time, as you see God move in your circumstances—providing breakthroughs, peace, or unexpected paths—you can record the ways He's answered. Perhaps you'll place a checkmark, write a date, or add a small note celebrating His faithfulness. These answered prayers serve as tangible markers of God's love and sovereignty in your life, reminding you that He truly does hear and respond. As the board fills up with testimonies of His goodness, it becomes more than just a record—it transforms into an altar of gratitude, a visual timeline of the many ways God has led, sustained, and delivered you according to His perfect timing and will. When doubts arise, revisiting this prayer board can fortify your faith, reinforcing that "He who promised is faithful" (Hebrews 10:23) and will continue to guide you through every season.

Questions for Reflection

1. What specific images or words reflect the future I believe God is preparing for me?
2. How can I use my vision board to pray intentionally over each dream?
3. In what ways can a dedicated prayer board help me track and celebrate God's answers throughout the year?

_____

_____

_____

_____

Prayer for Today

Lord, give me spiritual vision. Help me capture on paper (or in pictures) the dreams You've planted in my heart. May this vision board keep me focused and remind me of Your faithfulness. Amen.

Self-Affirmation

I see God's promises clearly before me and trust Him to bring them to pass.

DAY 12: BE ACCOUNTABLE

Scripture

"As iron sharpens iron, so a friend sharpens a friend." (Proverbs 27:17 NLT)

Devotion

Accountability is essential for growth. Proverbs 27:17 says, "As iron sharpens iron, so a friend sharpens a friend," reminding us that we thrive when we allow trusted people into our process—people who encourage us and lovingly correct us when we stray. Even Jesus sent the disciples out in pairs, illustrating that we weren't designed to walk alone. When you live in isolation, it's easier to procrastinate, give in to temptation, or lose sight of your commitments. You might have the best intentions, but without someone to check in, offer support, and challenge your excuses, even well-formed goals can fall by the wayside.

Accountability partners—whether friends, mentors, or a small group—are invaluable because they help keep your actions aligned with your words. When you share your goals and aspirations with someone who genuinely cares, you gain both a cheerleader and a coach. They can celebrate your victories, offering recognition and praise when you hit a milestone or take a courageous step forward. Yet they also stand ready to pray with you through challenges, bringing spiritual support and encouragement during moments of doubt or struggle. Moreover, an accountability partner speaks truth into your life when you're veering off course, offering loving correction that helps you realign with your values and commitments.

One of the greatest advantages of having such relationships is the safe, supportive space they create. Instead of hiding struggles behind pride or fear, you learn to be transparent about your shortcomings and aspirations. This vulnerability opens the door for genuine transformation, because real change thrives in environments where honesty is met with compassion—not judgment. The goals you once held privately become shared pursuits, guided by collective wisdom and mutual encouragement. Ecclesiastes 4:9–10 illustrates that "two are better than one" because they can lift each other up. In this kind of community, growth is not only possible but often accelerated, as each step forward is undergirded by prayers, practical advice, and the sincere belief that you can reach the God-given potential within you.

Questions for Reflection

1. Who do I trust to hold me accountable in my spiritual and personal goals?
2. Am I open to both encouragement and correction from them? If not, why?
3. How can I cultivate deeper accountability relationships that foster genuine transparency and growth?

Prayer for Today

Lord, bring the right people into my life who will challenge me to stay the course. Give me a humble heart to receive accountability and the courage to be transparent. In Jesus' name, amen.

Self-Affirmation

I welcome accountability as a tool for my growth and success.

DAY 13: SPEAK WHAT YOU KNOW

Scripture

"Let the redeemed of the Lord say so, whom He has redeemed from the hand of the enemy." (Psalm 107:2 NKJV)

Devotion

Your testimony has real power. Whether it's deliverance from fear, healing from brokenness, or a moment when God's grace became undeniably real in your life—speak it. The Bible often encourages us to "let the redeemed of the Lord say so" (Psalm 107:2), because declaring God's goodness not only reinforces your own faith but also has the power to inspire and uplift others who may be facing similar battles. When you share how God carried you through a difficult season, you shine a light on His faithfulness and help others see that if He did it for you, He can do it for them.

The enemy often tries to silence our testimonies by planting seeds of doubt, shame, or the insidious idea that our story isn't "important enough" to share. He knows that a spoken testimony carries great power—Revelation 12:11 reveals that "they overcame him by the blood of the Lamb and by the word of their testimony." When you boldly declare what the Lord has done in your life, you push back against the lies that say you should remain silent. Speaking your story breaks chains of fear and doubt, serving as a vivid reminder—to both you and those around you—that God is not just a distant figure but a present, active force in every detail of our lives. There's tangible victory in your voice when you proclaim His faithfulness, even in the seemingly smallest moments of provision or comfort.

Over time, each testimony you share builds spiritual momentum, creating a ripple effect of hope. This wave of faith can extend further than you might ever see firsthand, encouraging hearts, stirring others to believe for their own breakthroughs, and illuminating the reality that God continues to move powerfully in our modern world.

Questions for Reflection

1. What has God done for me recently that I can share?
2. How can my testimony encourage someone else to overcome?
3. What fears or doubts have kept me from sharing my story, and how can I address them with faith?

Prayer for Today

Lord, thank You for redeeming me. Give me the boldness to speak of Your goodness and the courage to share my testimony with others. Amen.

Self-Affirmation

I am redeemed, and I boldly share my story to glorify God.

DAY 14: BIND DISCOURAGEMENT

Scripture

"Why am I discouraged? Why is my heart so sad? I will put my hope in God!" (Psalm 42:11 NLT)

Devotion

Discouragement often sneaks in when our expectations aren't met, or obstacles feel overwhelming. It tempts us to quit, lose hope, or doubt God's promises, subtly planting the idea that things will never change. Yet the psalmist David, in moments of deep despair, shows us an alternative: "Why am I discouraged? Why is my heart so sad? I will put my hope in God!" (Psalm 42:5). This raw honesty paired with a deliberate refocusing on the Lord highlights a powerful truth—discouragement cannot coexist with hope. One will always drive out the other.

When you find discouragement creeping in, recognize it early and speak life to yourself. Remind your heart of every victory God has granted you, no matter how small it may seem in hindsight. Reflect on the times He guided you through tight spots, answered desperate prayers, or simply gave you peace in chaos. Each recollection becomes fuel against despair, reinforcing the truth that God's faithfulness persists in every season. Whether it's through journaling, prayer, or sharing testimonies with trusted friends, actively storing up God's track record of goodness helps you combat discouragement before it can take root. By intentionally shifting your mindset to hope and gratitude, you stand firm against the lies that say you should give up.

Questions for Reflection

1. What triggers discourage me the easiest?

2. How can I shift my mindset when I feel disappointment rising?

3. Which specific past victories or testimonies from my life can I recall right now to reignite my hope in God's promises?

Prayer for Today

Father, I bind every spirit of discouragement in my life. Replace it with renewed hope and faith. Help me to recall Your faithfulness in the past as a reminder that You will see me through again. Amen.

Self-Affirmation

My hope is in God. I refuse to let discouragement rule my heart.

DAY 15: WHO ARE YOUR FRIENDS?

Scripture

"Walk with the wise and become wise; associate with fools and get in trouble." (Proverbs 13:20 NLT)

Devotion

Friends have the power to influence us profoundly. Proverbs 13:20 states, "Walk with the wise and become wise; associate with fools and get in trouble," illustrating how the company we keep can propel us toward growth or lead us astray. If you feel you have few friends, take heart—quality truly does matter more than quantity. One or two God-honoring friends who speak truth, offer encouragement, and genuinely care about your spiritual well-being can far outweigh a crowd of superficial acquaintances. The depth of authentic friendship is often rooted in mutual respect, shared values, and a willingness to invest in each other's growth.

Ask God to bring people into your life who will strengthen your faith and inspire you to become more like Christ. At the same time, remain open to being that kind of friend for someone else. Authentic friendship is reciprocal; it thrives on love, honesty, and selflessness. Instead of fixating on how many friends you have, focus on cultivating deeper bonds with the few who are committed to walking alongside you in both the joys and the challenges of life. This might mean stepping out of your comfort zone—inviting someone to coffee, asking intentional questions, or offering support when they're going through a tough season. As you do, remember that

God sees your effort to love and be loved in healthy, uplifting relationships.

Questions for Reflection

1. Do my closest relationships reflect the values I want to nurture in my life?
2. How can I be a better friend to others?
3. In what ways can I remain open to new friendships or deepen existing ones, while maintaining healthy boundaries?

_____
_____
_____
_____
_____
_____
_____
_____
_____
_____
_____
_____
_____

Prayer for Today

Lord, bring the right friendships into my life—people who speak truth, love, and encouragement. Help me also be a friend who uplifts others. Even if I feel alone, remind me that I am never truly alone with You. Amen.

Self-Affirmation

I value friendships that encourage spiritual growth and mutual support.

DAY 16: POSTURE OF PRAYER

Scripture

"Never stop praying." (1 Thessalonians 5:17 NLT)

Devotion

Prayer is more than an event; it's a posture of the heart—a continuous communion with God that goes far beyond quick mealtime blessings or bedtime routines. 1 Thessalonians 5:17 encourages believers to "never stop praying," underscoring that prayer isn't merely a scheduled activity but a moment-by-moment connection with our Creator. Yes, it's valuable to set aside dedicated times for prayer—quiet mornings in God's Word, meditative walks, or evening reflections—yet cultivating the habit of conversing with Him in the ordinary moments (while driving, working, cooking, or even waiting in line) transforms daily routines into sacred spaces.

This posture of ongoing prayer is a humble acknowledgment that we need God in every moment, not just when problems arise. It also changes how we perceive our circumstances. Instead of compartmentalizing life into "spiritual" and "non-spiritual" sections, we begin seeing God's fingerprints everywhere. From asking for guidance before a crucial decision to silently thanking Him for a burst of inspiration at work, prayer keeps our hearts tethered to His presence. Over time, this constant, open line to heaven fosters both trust in His sovereignty and sensitivity to His Spirit's leading. It shifts our reliance from self to the One who sustains us, allowing us to face each day's challenges with renewed hope and peace.

Questions for Reflection

1. Do I limit prayer to certain times, or is it woven into my everyday life?

2. How can I deepen my awareness of God's presence throughout my day?

3. In what practical ways can I remind myself to pray continuously, especially in the mundane or busy moments?

Prayer for Today

Heavenly Father, keep my heart in a posture of prayer. Let my first response to any situation be communication with You. Transform my life through a deeper, ongoing relationship with You. Amen.

Self-Affirmation

Prayer is my lifestyle. I connect with God in every moment.

DAY 17: FUELED WITH FAITH

Scripture

- "But they delight in the law of the Lord, meditating on it day and night." (Psalm 1:2 NLT)

- "Fix your thoughts on what is true, and honorable, and right, and pure, and lovely, and admirable." (Philippians 4:8 NLT)

Devotion

Faith is fueled by what you meditate on. If you constantly dwell on negativity, doubt, and fear, your faith will naturally struggle to stay afloat—much like a boat taking on water. Conversely, if you fill your mind with God's Word, positive declarations, and testimonies of His goodness, your faith will flourish. Philippians 4:8 tells us to fix our thoughts on "whatever is true, noble, right, pure, lovely, and admirable," reminding us that our focus plays a critical role in shaping our beliefs and attitudes.

Just as a car needs consistent refueling to keep running smoothly, you must regularly refill your heart with faith-building content. Whether through listening to worship music, reading Scripture each morning, or sharing testimonies of God's faithfulness with friends, these practices keep your spiritual "tank" from running dry. Consider the environment you create for yourself—both online and offline—and assess whether it aligns with the faith you're trying to nurture. When you intentionally surround yourself with godly influences, your perspective shifts from pessimism to hope, and from fear to trust in the One who holds all things together.

Questions for Reflection

1. What am I fueling my mind with daily—fearful media or faith-filled truths?

2. Which spiritual disciplines can I commit to that will strengthen my faith?

3. How can I reshape my daily routines or environments to consistently nourish my soul with life-giving content?

Prayer for Today

Lord, I desire to be fueled by faith, not fear. Help me to delight in Your Word and fix my thoughts on what is godly and uplifting. Strengthen my faith day by day. Amen.

Self-Affirmation

I choose to feed my heart with God's truth, fueling my faith for every challenge.

DAY 18: RESTORATION OF IDEAS

Scripture

"I will restore to you the years that the swarming locust has eaten." (Joel 2:25 ESV)

Devotion

Sometimes, disappointments and failures can make us feel that all our creative ideas or dreams have been lost. A significant setback—like missing a key opportunity or experiencing a painful rejection—can lead us to abandon visions we once held dear. Yet Joel 2:25 promises that God will "restore the years that the swarming locust has eaten," reminding us that He specializes in bringing renewal where we see only loss. The dreams or ideas you've shelved due to disillusionment can still have a future; God can breathe life back into them, reigniting a passion you thought was gone for good.

Ask Him to revive any dream or idea He still intends for you to pursue. He is able to multiply your time, resources, and abilities to accomplish His will, even if it feels like you're starting from scratch. What once seemed irretrievable can be revived under God's restorative hand, sometimes returning in an even stronger or more refined form than you originally imagined. Trust that your season of waiting or disappointment wasn't wasted—it was fertile ground for God to prepare you, shape your character, and ready the circumstances for a fresh beginning.

Questions for Reflection

1. What dreams or ideas have I abandoned due to setbacks or discouragement?

2. How can I invite God to restore and breathe new life into them?

3. In what ways have my setbacks prepared me for a more fruitful relaunch of those dreams?

Prayer for Today

Father, thank You for being a God of restoration. Revive the dreams and ideas You've placed in my heart. May they be used for Your glory. In Jesus' name, amen.

Self-Affirmation

Nothing is truly lost when placed in God's hands—He restores all things in His time.

DAY 19: END PROCRASTINATION

Scripture

"A little sleep, a little slumber, a little folding of the hands to rest—and poverty will come on you like a thief." (Proverbs 24:33-34 NIV)

Devotion

Procrastination often stems from fear—fear of failure, fear of not being good enough, or fear of stepping into the unknown. We push tasks aside, hoping a more convenient time will come, only to discover that the "perfect time" rarely arrives. The result is often a mounting sense of anxiety that feeds the very fears we're trying to avoid. 2 Timothy 1:7 reminds us that God does not give us a spirit of fear but of power, love, and sound judgment, underscoring that our natural hesitations don't have to dictate our actions.

Still, the cycle of avoidance can feel paralyzing. Each day that passes without progress makes our responsibilities appear more daunting, reinforcing the notion that we aren't capable or prepared enough to tackle them. Overthinking about potential worst-case scenarios or wrestling with the fear of disappointing others can lead us to do nothing at all. But Ephesians 2:10 testifies that God has prepared good works for us in advance, indicating that we're not only called but also equipped to overcome the obstacles on our path.

Breaking the cycle starts with small, intentional steps. Perhaps it's sorting a cluttered closet, sending that important email, or initiating a hard but necessary conversation—each step of obedience, however modest, chips away at procrastination's grip. As you surrender your fear to God and trust in His empowerment, you'll find that consistent, faithful action eventually displaces the paralyzing refrain of "maybe later." Over time, you'll see tangible progress unfolding—a reflection of both God's grace and your willingness to lean on His strength rather than succumbing to fear.

Questions for Reflection

1. What important tasks or goals have I been putting off and why?

2. How can I break a large goal into smaller, manageable steps?

3. In what ways can relying on God's power help me overcome the fear that fuels procrastination?

Prayer for Today

Lord, help me overcome the fear or laziness behind my procrastination. Give me the motivation to start, the discipline to continue, and the faith to finish what You've called me to do. Amen.

Self-Affirmation

I will take action today! I will not let fear or doubt delay my progress.

DAY 20: SO, WHAT IT DIDN'T WORK THE 1ST TIME

Scripture

"Come to Me, all you who labor and are heavy laden, and I will give you rest." (Matthew 11:28-30 NKJV)

Devotion

Failing on the first try can feel overwhelming, especially when you've invested time, energy, or even your emotional well-being into pursuing a goal. Yet Psalm 37:23–24 reminds us that though we stumble, we will not be utterly cast down because the Lord holds us up. God never intended for you to carry the weight of perfection on your shoulders; instead, He invites you to release that burden and learn from each misstep. In His grace, there is room for growth, adjustment, and a fresh perspective. Whether it's a career setback, a relationship disappointment, or a ministry challenge, every experience—good or bad—can be a stepping stone on the path to deeper maturity.

When something doesn't work out as planned, it's not the end of the story. God can use detours to develop perseverance, character, and a greater trust in His ways (Romans 5:3–4). Failure is often a teacher, not a final verdict. Dust yourself off and try again—this time with God's direction and peace, knowing that He can bring beauty even from the ashes of disappointment. Embracing this mindset not only lifts the weight of perfectionism but also positions you to see the bigger picture of how God's faithfulness can turn setbacks into testimonies of His redemptive power.

Questions for Reflection

1. How can I view failure as a learning opportunity rather than a final defeat?

2. What burden am I carrying alone that I need to surrender to God?

3. In what ways might my setbacks be shaping my character or strengthening my relationship with the Lord?

_____

_____

_____

_____

_____

_____

_____

_____

_____

_____

_____

_____

_____

_____

Prayer for Today

Jesus, thank You for inviting me to lay down my burdens. Teach me to see failed attempts as steppingstones in Your plan for my growth. Renew my resolve to keep moving forward with faith. Amen.

Self-Affirmation

A setback is not my ending. I will learn, adapt, and keep going by God's grace.

DAY 21: KNOWLEDGE PLUS EXPERIENCE EQUALS EXPERTISE

Scripture

"Give instruction to a wise man, and he will be still wiser; teach a righteous man, and he will increase in learning." (Proverbs 9:9 ESV)

Devotion

Knowledge alone isn't enough; it must be applied! When you combine what you've learned (knowledge) with real-life action (experience), you develop true expertise. This principle applies to every facet of life, including spiritual matters. James 1:22 cautions us to be doers of the Word, not merely hearers, reminding us that hearing truth without putting it into practice accomplishes little. Knowing Scripture is indeed the foundation, but living it out—through love, service, forgiveness, and humility—creates the transformation that touches your life and the lives of those around you.

Ask yourself: What have I learned in my journey that I can now teach or share? Sometimes, the hardships, lessons, and small victories you've accumulated over the years become the very testimonies someone else needs to hear. You never know how your experience can serve as a guidepost for someone else seeking direction, hope, or encouragement. Applying knowledge also fosters continual growth; as you step out in faith and practice what you've learned, you solidify those lessons, shaping not just your own character but potentially impacting entire communities.

Questions for Reflection

1. What specific knowledge do I already have that could help me—and others—if I applied it more consistently?

2. Am I willing to share my experiences and lessons learned with those who might benefit? If not, why not?

3. In what areas of my life can I transform theoretical knowledge into practical action this week?

Prayer for Today

Lord, grant me the wisdom to apply what I learn and the humility to share my experiences for Your glory. Turn my knowledge into practical service and my experiences into testimonies. Amen.

Self-Affirmation

I am growing wiser each day as I apply my knowledge and experiences for God's purposes.

DAY 22: DON'T LET THE PAST CREEP UP ON YOU

Scripture

- "For all the promises of God in Him are Yes, and in Him Amen." (2 Corinthians 1:20 NKJV)

- "Therefore, having these promises, beloved, let us cleanse ourselves." (2 Corinthians 7:1 NKJV)

- "See, I have this day set you over the nations and over the kingdoms, to root out and to pull down… to build and to plant." (Jeremiah 1:10 NKJV)

Devotion

Your past, including your failures and shortcomings, can be a powerful testimony—but it can also be a trap if you let shame and regret creep back in. Romans 8:28 assures us that God works all things together for the good of those who love Him, which means your past can be repurposed for His glory. Whether it's mistakes you've made or hurts you've endured, God is fully capable of redeeming them to shape you into who He's called you to be. However, you must guard against letting old memories or destructive patterns resurface in a way that hinders your current growth. If you dwell too long on yesterday's regrets, you miss the new opportunities God is placing before you today.

You can use your past experiences to help others overcome, but only if you're not bound by them yourself. Staying vigilant means recognizing distractions or old habits that try to pull you off course and then consciously choosing a different path. Philippians 3:13–14 reminds us to forget what lies behind and strain forward to what lies ahead. If God has broken old chains in your life, stand firm in that freedom. Be quick to refocus on His promises, allowing Him to transform every mistake, wound, or misstep into a testimony of His grace. In doing so, you become a living witness, able to encourage those who may be stuck where you once were.

Questions for Reflection

1. What recurring thoughts or habits from the past threaten my present growth?

2. How can I use my testimony of overcoming the past to uplift others?

3. What specific promises from God's Word can I cling to when old shame or regret tries to creep back in?

_____
_____
_____
_____
_____
_____
_____
_____
_____
_____

Prayer for Today

Lord, help me see my past as a testimony of Your grace, not a chain of shame. Guard my mind against old distractions. Let me serve others by sharing how You've delivered me. Amen.

Self-Affirmation

My past is redeemed. I live in God's promises and use my story to bring hope to others.

DAY 23: HANDLE YOUR BUSINESS

Scripture

"Whatever you do, work at it with all your heart, as though you were working for the Lord and not for people." (Colossians 3:23 GNT)

Devotion

God cares about every aspect of your life, including the practical responsibilities—finances, career, and daily tasks—that might seem mundane or secular. When Scripture calls us to do everything for the glory of God (1 Corinthians 10:31), it doesn't exclude the everyday details. "Handling your business" means approaching your commitments with integrity, diligence, and excellence. In doing so, you transform ordinary tasks into acts of worship, as you recognize that everything you have—time, resources, skills—comes from God and ultimately belongs to Him.

Sometimes, we over-spiritualize certain parts of life (like church attendance or Bible study) while neglecting others (like paying bills on time or managing our workload). But God is holistic in His approach to us. He cares about your prayer life and how you manage your finances. He's interested in your spiritual growth and your work ethic. By stewarding well what He has entrusted to you, you demonstrate gratitude and honor for the Giver of every good gift. When you treat your daily responsibilities as opportunities to serve and reflect God's character—rather than just chores or obligations—you'll discover a deeper sense of purpose and fulfillment in every corner of your life.

Questions for Reflection

1. In what areas do I need more diligence or integrity (finances, work ethic, time management)?

2. How can I reframe my daily tasks as acts of worship?

3. What practical changes—such as scheduling, budgeting, or accountability—could help me better steward my responsibilities to the glory of God?

Prayer for Today

Lord, help me to handle my responsibilities with integrity and excellence. May I do all things as unto You, reflecting Your character in my work and daily tasks. Amen.

Self-Affirmation

I handle my responsibilities diligently, reflecting God's excellence in everything I do.

DAY 24: SWIFT OBEDIENCE

Scripture

"If you love Me, keep My commandments." (John 14:15 NKJV)

Devotion

Delayed obedience can lead to missed opportunities or prolonged struggles. Sometimes, we sense God's prompting—maybe through Scripture, a sermon, or the Holy Spirit speaking to our hearts—but we hesitate, second-guessing our own readiness or God's timing. Yet 1 Samuel 15:22 reminds us that obedience is better than sacrifice, pointing out that God values a willing heart that responds to His voice. Swift obedience not only demonstrates trust and love for Him but also shows that we take His direction seriously enough to act on it without delay.

Consider biblical figures like Abraham, who left his homeland at God's command without even knowing his destination (Hebrews 11:8). His immediate response set the stage for God's miraculous interventions and abundant blessings. Similarly, the disciples left their nets to follow Jesus at once (Matthew 4:20). Their willingness to move quickly signaled a commitment to place God's agenda above their own. Let these examples inspire you to follow God's leading with urgency and faith, trusting that He sees the bigger picture—even when you don't.

Questions for Reflection

1. In what areas of my life have I been slow to obey God's leading?

2. How can I practice responding to His voice more quickly?

3. What practical steps or mindset shifts can help me overcome hesitations and align my actions with God's promptings?

Prayer for Today

Father, give me a heart that delights in swift obedience. Remove any hesitation, fear, or pride. Help me follow Your commands as a clear demonstration of my love for You. Amen.

Self-Affirmation

I respond quickly to God's direction, trusting His perfect plan for my life.

DAY 25: GROW WHERE YOU ARE PLANTED

Scripture

"Those who are planted in the house of the Lord shall flourish in the courts of our God." (Psalm 92:13 NKJV)

Devotion

Alright… we are 25 days in… you may feel like you are doing well—making progress but still not at the speed you may like resulting in feeling a little discontented. Remember, discontentment can trick us into believing we must be elsewhere, doing something else, to truly thrive. Yet God often calls us to blossom right where He has assigned us—even if it's challenging or not our ideal situation. Jeremiah 17:7–8 paints a picture of a tree planted by the waters, flourishing regardless of external circumstances. In the same way, when you commit to growing where you're planted, you learn invaluable lessons about faithfulness, perseverance, and gratitude. You begin to see that the conditions aren't as important as the One who sustains you.

Sometimes, we hold tightly to dreams that involve being anywhere but our current location—whether it's a different job, city, or life stage. But if God wants to move you, He will direct your steps clearly at the right time. Until then, water the seeds He's given you now by pouring your heart and energy into your present responsibilities, relationships, and spiritual growth. As you do, you'll discover that He can bring fruitfulness even in places you once considered barren. Embracing this truth not only fosters contentment but also positions you to receive unexpected blessings that might have been overlooked if your focus were elsewhere.

Questions for Reflection

1. Have I been longing to be somewhere else instead of stewarding my current place well?
2. How can I show faithfulness and excellence where God has me now?
3. In what ways has God already demonstrated His ability to bring growth and blessing in challenging or unexpected environments?

Prayer for Today

Lord, help me to be faithful in my current season. Teach me to flourish where You've planted me. Give me patience and trust in Your timing for any changes ahead. Amen.

Self-Affirmation

I flourish where God has placed me, trusting His wisdom for my season.

DAY 26: BIND IMPATIENCE... WHILE YOU WAIT

Scripture

Read Psalm 62 & Psalm 27

Devotion

You may find yourself saying, "Lord, you asked me to "Try Again" but this is taking TOOOOOO long." We must remember that waiting is challenging, especially when it feels like everyone else is moving forward while you remain in place. Impatience can tempt us to take shortcuts or make hasty decisions that ultimately derail our progress. Yet Scripture encourages us time and again to "wait on the Lord." This isn't passive waiting; it's an active posture of faith that trusts God's sovereignty and timing. Isaiah 40:31 reminds us that those who wait on the Lord "shall renew their strength," suggesting that God often uses waiting seasons to refine our character, sharpen our focus, and deepen our reliance on Him.

God sees unlimited potential in you, even if others have dismissed or overlooked you. 2 Corinthians 1:20 declares that all His promises are "Yes" in Christ, indicating that He is steadfast and will fulfill His word in due time. During periods of waiting, it can be easy to doubt your value or become anxious about the future but remember that God's timeline is both purposeful and redemptive. Use this season as a time for preparation and growth… whether that's delving into Scripture, honing a skill set, or cultivating a more profound prayer life. As you align your heart with God's promises, you'll find that this waiting season is less about delay and more about the spiritual groundwork needed for the journey ahead.

Questions for Reflection

1. In what areas of life am I most impatient?

2. How can I better utilize my waiting season for spiritual growth?

3. What specific Scriptures or promises can I meditate on to cultivate greater trust in God's timing?

_____
_____
_____
_____
_____
_____
_____
_____
_____
_____
_____
_____
_____

Prayer for Today

Lord, I surrender my timeline to You. Teach me patience. When I feel tempted to rush ahead, remind me of Your faithfulness. Use my waiting season to prepare me for the blessings You have in store. Amen.

Self-Affirmation

I trust God's perfect timing. My waiting season is a time of growth, not a setback.

DAY 27: ARE YOU PREPARED?

Scripture

"Therefore, you also be ready, for the Son of Man is coming at an hour you do not expect." (Matthew 24:44 NKJV)

Devotion

Preparedness isn't just about end times; it's about daily readiness to respond to God's call. Matthew 24:44 urges us to "be ready," but this principle stretches well beyond apocalyptic warnings. It's also about being prepared in the everyday moments—ready to share your faith, step into a ministry opportunity, or extend compassion to someone who needs hope. Are you prepared spiritually—rooted in prayer and grounded in God's Word—so that when He nudges you, you can respond confidently? And are you prepared practically, having done the necessary work or study for that new role or open-door God might orchestrate?

Readiness aligns with faith. If you genuinely believe God can move suddenly or open a door unexpectedly, you'll live in a posture of expectancy—keeping your spiritual eyes open and your heart prepared. Instead of passively waiting for a "perfect time," you'll continually cultivate your walk with God, refine your skills, and remain sensitive to the Holy Spirit's leading. Through this constant state of preparedness, you'll not only seize God-ordained moments but also grow deeper in your relationship with Him, recognizing His hand in every opportunity that comes your way.

Questions for Reflection

1. Am I living each day expecting God to speak, lead, and open doors?

2. How am I positioning myself—spiritually and practically—for opportunities from God?

3. In what ways can I keep building daily habits that keep my heart and mind in a state of ongoing preparedness?

Prayer for Today

Lord, help me live in constant readiness. Shape my heart and mind to be receptive to Your voice and prepared for divine appointments. In Jesus' name, amen.

Self-Affirmation

I am ready to respond when God calls, prepared both spiritually and practically.

DAY 28: CALIBRATING FOR CONTINUAL SUCCESS

Scripture

"Examine yourselves to see if your faith is genuine. Test yourselves." (2 Corinthians 13:5 NLT)

Devotion

Calibration is more than a one-time action; it's a commitment to regularly check and adjust our spiritual and practical lives. In the same way a compass needs to be aligned to ensure accurate navigation, our hearts need periodic alignment with God's Word to stay on course. 2 Corinthians 13:5 instructs us to "examine yourselves to see if your faith is genuine," emphasizing the importance of self-reflection. When we take time to assess our motives, behaviors, and thought patterns, we allow the Holy Spirit to illuminate areas in need of transformation, ensuring we remain effective in what God has called us to do.

True success—both spiritually and practically—doesn't just happen. It's the product of consistent growth and willingness to adjust. Life's hustle can gradually push our priorities out of order: distractions creep in, old habits resurface, or fatigue weakens our resolve. By intentionally recalibrating, we acknowledge we're never "done" growing. Instead, each season presents fresh opportunities to refine our focus and deepen our commitment. Romans 12:2 reminds us not to conform to the patterns of this world but to be transformed by the renewing of our minds—an ongoing process that aligns us with God's will, leading to a fruitful life.

Remember, recalibration isn't a sign of failure; it's a proactive measure that keeps us on a trajectory of continual success. Whether it involves setting aside regular time for prayer and Scripture study, seeking wise counsel, or journaling about where we might have drifted, these intentional steps help us maintain spiritual sharpness. As we cooperate with God's gentle corrections, He reshapes our desires, revitalizes our vision, and empowers us to navigate life's challenges from a place of strength and clarity.

Questions for Reflection

1. Where in my life might I need recalibration right now?
2. What daily or weekly habits can I establish to ensure I'm regularly checking my alignment with God's Word?
3. How can I incorporate accountability or community support in my regular process of spiritual calibration?

Prayer for Today

Father, search my heart and show me where I need realignment. Give me the humility to make changes and the discipline to maintain a lifestyle in sync with Your will. Amen.

Self-Affirmation

I pause to recalibrate and realign my heart, ensuring I walk in God's truth.

DAY 29: PAY IT FORWARD

Scripture

"Freely you have received; freely give." (Matthew 10:8 NIV)

Devotion

God blesses us so that we can be a blessing to others—whether by sharing encouragement, financial resources, or our time and talents. This principle of "paying it forward" reflects God's heart of generosity and breaks self-centered cycles that can keep us focused only on our own needs. As this is Day 29 and you have been on this journey and we know that when you extend kindness, you help foster a culture of compassion and community care. Acts 20:35 reminds us that it is more blessed to give than to receive, reinforcing that our blessings become truly meaningful when they bless someone else.

Take a moment to recall someone who has poured into your life—perhaps a mentor, friend, or even a stranger who offered you support at a critical time. Remember how their generosity made you feel seen, valued, and hopeful. Now, imagine being that same instrument of blessing for someone else. Every time you invest your resources, time, or words of affirmation in another person, you reflect the very nature of God, who is the ultimate giver. John 3:16 shows us the depth of His giving heart; when we "pay it forward," we echo that love in tangible ways. Over time, this lifestyle of generosity not only benefits those you help, but also enriches your own relationship with God and others.

Questions for Reflection

1. As I have been motivated to be "whole" over the last 29 days; who can I bless or help with my time, resources, or knowledge this week?

2. How can "paying it forward" become a consistent habit rather than a one-time act?

3. What simple, daily practices can I incorporate to keep generosity at the forefront of my thoughts and actions?

Prayer for Today

Lord, give me a heart of generosity. Show me opportunities to bless others as You have blessed me. Let my giving point people toward Your loving kindness. Amen.

Self-Affirmation

I am blessed to be a blessing. I freely give as I have freely received.

DAY 30: REDEMPTIVE LOVE!

Scripture

"But God demonstrates His own love toward us, in that while we were still sinners, Christ died for us." (Romans 5:8 NKJV)

Devotion

God's redemptive love is the cornerstone of our faith. It doesn't wait for us to be perfect or worthy; it meets us in our brokenness and lifts us to new life. Romans 5:8 tells us that while we were still sinners, Christ died for us—an unfathomable display of love that shows the depth of God's commitment to redeem us. Throughout this 30-day journey, you've explored how God's grace reaches into every failure, every disappointment, and every fear, reshaping them into stepping stones toward growth and wholeness. No matter where you started, you can stand assured that your life bears witness to His redemptive power.

As you conclude this devotional, remember that "Try Again" isn't just a catchy phrase—it's an invitation to continually lean into God's grace, to learn from every stumble, and to experience wholeness through His redemptive love. Lamentations 3:22–23 reminds us that His mercies are new every morning, signaling that we always have an opportunity to rise again, wiser and stronger than before. The end of these 30 days marks the beginning of a lifelong adventure of trusting God's redeeming work in every facet of your life—relationships, career, ministry, and personal growth. Where you've seen His love restore and revive, take it as evidence that nothing is beyond His power to heal.

Questions for Reflection

1. In what ways have I experienced God's redemptive love over the past 30 days?

2. How can I remain anchored in this truth even after this devotional ends?

3. What practical steps can I take to share God's redemptive love with others in my daily life?

Prayer for Today

Father, thank You for loving me enough to redeem every part of my story. May I walk forward in wholeness, continually reminded that Your love transforms and restores. In Jesus' name, amen.

Self-Affirmation

I am redeemed, loved, and empowered by Christ's sacrifice. My journey to wholeness continues daily in Him.

Conclusion & Next Steps

You've made it through these 30 days of reflection, prayer, and growth… Congratulations! This journey was never about perfection. Instead, it was about learning to TRY AGAIN each time you stumble. It was about facing your fears, confronting hard truths, and inviting God to transform every area of your life… your family, career, ministry, and personal ambitions.

Keep the Momentum Going

Revisit Your Journal

Look back on the notes, prayers, and reflections you recorded over the past month. Notice patterns, themes, and areas where God clearly showed up. Let these reminders encourage you whenever you feel stuck or discouraged again.

Refine Your Goals and Vision

Take time to revisit your original goals or prayer/vision board. Which goals have become clearer? Which ones need revision or expansion? Pray for continued direction, and trust that God will guide you to Try Again if any path seems unclear.

Stay Accountable

Share your progress with a trusted friend, mentor, or small group. Accountability helps you stay focused and provides fresh perspectives. Don't hesitate to ask others to pray for you, check in on your progress, or offer practical support.

Build on New Habits

Any habit - prayer, devotional reading, time management - becomes more powerful when practiced consistently. Continue cultivating the patterns you've started. Whether it's morning prayer, weekly goal-setting, or scheduled rest days, see these disciplines as long-term investments in your spiritual and emotional health.

Embrace Your Story

Your journey, complete with missteps and victories, is uniquely yours. Use it to encourage someone else who might be struggling. Sharing your testimony can strengthen your own faith as well as spark hope in others.

A Final Word of Encouragement

Remember, TRYING AGAIN doesn't end here. Life will bring new challenges, successes, and unexpected turns. Through it all, keep pressing forward, confident that you are growing in WHOLEness day by day. If you ever feel overwhelmed or uncertain, PLEASE revisit these devotionals, scripture references, and prayers. Allow Holy Spirit to remind you of God's steadfast love and the promises He has for your life so you can be whole!

Whether your goals involve healing family relationships, advancing in your career, or stepping boldly into ministry, don't lose sight of the core truth: God is with you every step of the way. Each time you stumble, His grace is sufficient to help you TRY AGAIN. Then, each time you encounter success, remember to give Him the glory.

As you leave this 30-day journey, go forward with expectation, hope, and renewed vision. You are loved, you are equipped, and you are called—so keep going, keep growing, and keep trusting in the Lord who makes all things possible.

"Being confident of this very thing, that He who has begun a good work in you will complete it until the day of Jesus Christ."
(Philippians 1:6 NKJV)

Now, go forward and live out the fullness of WHOLEness you've been discovering. The best is yet to come!

About the Author

Dr. Casaundra Monique Steward-McNair is a dedicated lifelong educator with a diverse career spanning over 20 years in both educational and ministry roles. Her commitment to serving and empowering communities is evident through her extensive work in various educational settings and her active involvement in church leadership.

Dr. McNair began her career as a preschool teacher and has served as a middle school teacher, Principal at all levels, Special Education Coordinator, Director of Diversity, Equity and Inclusion, Director of Special Education and Adjunct Professor.

She holds a Bachelor of Arts in Liberal Studies, a Master of Arts in Special Education, a Master of Arts in Educational Administration, and a Doctoral Degree in Leadership for Educational Justice.

Alongside her husband, Dr. McNair co-founded The Rhema House, serves as the CEO of The McNair Co, where she is the Chief Consultant, driven by her passion for educating and empowering underserved populations and churches; as well as the co-founder of We Blend, assisting blending families in thriving where they are. She often states, "transformative leadership is what is required to truly transform churches and educational environments."

Dr. McNair and her husband are blessed with three young adults: Devin, DeShun, and Dejah. Her personal and professional life is a testament to her unwavering commitment to education, ministry, and transformative leadership.

For more information…

www.themcnairco.org

www.ingramcontent.com/pod-product-compliance
Lightning Source LLC
Chambersburg PA
CBHW040748020526
44118CB00041B/2769